I Heard You Twice the First Time
Poems for Tired and Bewildered Teachers

by Kalli Dakos

With contributions by:
Sid Cratzbarg
Julia Critchfield
Tricia Gibbons
Eowana Jordan
Jan Price

Illustrations by
Denis Proulx
(cover, IBTIA Degree)

Graphic Design and all other
illustrations by Gina Marin

I Heard You Twice the First Time
Poems for Tired and Bewildered Teachers

ISBN: 1-4392-6148-2

Some poems in this text
(by Kalli Dakos)
were first published
by Scholastic, Inc.
THE GREATEST MAGIC
POEMS FOR TEACHERS
May, 2000

Printed in the USA
ISBN: 1-4392-6148-2
Library of Congress Control Number:
2010904629

Summary: A collection of humorous and inspirational poems
for tired and bewildered teachers.

Published by Edstar, Inc.

Dedication

This book is dedicated to the memory of Tricia Gibbons, who was an exceptional teacher, a wonderful poet and a dear friend. She spent more time listening to the music of the stars and the call of the wind than anyone I've ever known.

When Tricia became seriously ill, she kept her spirits high and her thoughts hopeful by calling her brain tumors "flowers" and by writing poems for the doctors who tried to save her life. She died in the summer of 2008.

Tricia had a deep friendship with poetry. She'd turn to words when life was difficult and challenging, and she wrote poems to celebrate the special moments and occasions of her life. This poem was written in honor of Tricia and the place poetry had in her life.

She Wrote the Poems

When grief had made
Her music still,
She wrote the poems
Of good and ill.

When pain came by
With twists and turns,
She wrote the poems
So she may learn.

When haunting fears
Played their part,
She wrote the poems
To steel her heart.

When love and joy
Shone so bright,
She wrote the poems
To save the light.

And now in pain
And through a blur,
I write this poem
With grief for her.

Introduction

These poems were inspired by author visits to countless schools in the United States and Canada over the past twenty years and my career as a teacher, reading specialist and poet of the school world.

There are also contributions by five wonderful teacher/librarian/poets – Sid Cratzbarg, Julia Critchfield, Tricia Gibbons, Eowana Jordan and Jan Price.

So many teachers have graciously shared their classroom stories with me, and I have spent countless hours in faculty rooms laughing and crying about life in our schools today.

I found dedicated, professional, hard-working teachers, struggling against all odds in every school I visited. They all had stories to share.

One teacher in New York told me that she had so many demands on her schedule that there was little time to "enjoy the joy" in her classroom. A teacher in Virginia shared a comment by one of her first graders after a hectic day in school. "I think we are all dying of seriousness," the little girl said.

When I visit a school, I do not look for high test scores, amazing technology or state-of-the-art teaching products. I look for the "spirit of childhood" and educators who are given time to "enjoy the joy."

I have written over 2,000 poems about life in school, but these are the most important words about education that I have ever put on paper:

> When we teach
> From within
> The spirit of childhood,
> We have our greatest power
> As educators.

This book is dedicated to teachers everywhere who have not forgotten the music of childhood and who bring its spirit into their classrooms.

Kalli Dakos,
January, 2010

Table of Contents

Poems for Tired Teachers

If you're tired
Come with me,
And read
A little poetry.

You'll find a place
To rest your soul,
And feel once more
The teacher's goal…

To pass the torch
In the dark,
To be the flame
That lights the heart,

To teach lessons
Of real worth,
For the journey here
On Planet Earth.

For the mystery
That's too big to see,
Except, perhaps,
Through poetry.

If you're tired
Come with me,
We're searching for
Our destiny.

Definition of Teachers

Astronauts,
Exploring
The far reaches
Of the universe
Inside of students.

Engineers,
Designing
Spaceships
Strong enough
To carry children
On their journey
Through life.

Scientists,
Studying
The minds
And hopes
And dreams
Of the earth's
Most precious resource.

Lost

Sometimes
I am lost
In the noise
And confusion
And chaos
Of the things

That don't matter.

I forget
To take time
To reflect
And wonder
And search my soul
For wisdom
And grace
And love
To guide me
To the things

That do matter.

A Rest in Childhood

Toys,
And old-fashioned playtime,
Spark imaginations,
Build creativity,
Nourish young souls,
And give children
A respite
From the madly-paced
Adult world,

*So they can rest
In childhood.*

They Put a Band-Aid on My Head

They put a Band-Aid on my head
And said I wasn't well,
They sent me to a special class
To read and write and spell.

I felt as if my brain
Was as dark as the sea,
Until I met the teacher
Who changed my life for me.

In her class we talked a lot,
We read, we wrote, we played,
And slowly, oh so slowly,
The pain began to fade.

When she took the Band-Aid off,
I was shocked to find,
There wasn't a bruise
Or even a scar,
No sore of any kind.

You Are My Friend

A circle is round
And has no end.
You are my teacher,
And my best friend.

A Head that Always Aches

Thirty kids!
You must be kidding,
In one classroom
Is absurd.
On other planets
Such a thought
Would be totally
Unheard.

Thirty kids!
All so active,
Is too much
To endure.
Ask a student,
Ask a teacher,
They'll agree,
I am quite sure.

Thirty kids!
And so much learning,
ABC's to
Book reports,
They need peace,
They need quiet,
All their thoughts
They need to sort.

Thirty kids!
In one classroom
Means a head that
Always aches.
Someone goofed
On this planet,
Some fool made
A big mistake.

Thirty kids!
Is too many,
In a class
You **must** agree.

If you don't,
Take my class,
Teach a day,

And you will see!

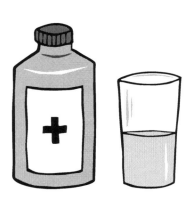

I Heard You Twice the First Time

(Teacher Talking to the Class)

I heard you twice the first time,
There is no need to shout!
I get the point,
I understand,
I KNOW the lights went out!

Time to Play

There are 86,400 seconds
In a day,
Use some of them for poetry,
And some of them to

Play!

The Greatest Magic

The greatest magic in the land,
Are books you hold in your hand.

A... B... C... D... E... F... G,
Letters wider than the sea,

H... I... J... K... L... and M,
More precious than the rarest gem,

N... O... P... Q... R... S... T,
Letters that can set you free,

U... V... W... X... Y... Z,
All of this I guarantee.

Twenty-six so small and light
But full of pictures clear and bright,

To take you on uncharted seas,
To laugh, to cry, to chase the breeze,

To travel time to futures past,
People die, but letters last.

Only twenty-six in all,
Squiggles on a paper scrawled,

That make a word, a thought, a hope,
A story, a prayer, a tear, a joke,

Inspire us so we may see,
All that we were meant to be.

Look at the gold in A,B,C,
And all the letters right to Z,

Read and see their sun shine bright,
Guides in the dark,
Stars in the night.

The Best Thing I Can Say
About My Teacher

She didn't care
As much about
Page 55,
As she did
About

ME!

A Teacher Stood at the Pearly Gates

A teacher stood at the Pearly Gates,
Her head was bent and low,
She only asked the man at the gate
Which way she had to go.

"What have you done," Saint Peter asked,
"To gain admittance here?"

"I taught school on earth," she sighed,
"For many and many a year."

Saint Peter opened wide the gates
And gently tolled the bell,
"Come in and choose your harp," he said.
"You've had your share of hell."

* This poem was adapted from a poem by anonymous.
  I found it on a wall in a pub in England and revised it for teachers

The Parent's Showing

by Julia Critichfield

Parents teach with ups and downs,
They give a child both smiles and frowns,
The seeds they plant are always growing,
Sometimes in school, the parent's showing.

Monkey see and monkey do,
If you hit me, then I'll hit too!
They learn at home, while they are growing,
Sometimes in school, the parent's showing.

Moms and dads must work, it's true,
They often have too much to do.
We see the seeds that they are sowing,
Sometimes in school, the parent's showing.

Like the moon that shines at night,
A child reflects the parent's light,
Or darkness or a full-moon glowing,
Sometimes in school, the parent's showing.

Stop the Clock

Stop the clock!
Take it down off the wall.
Sit on those
Silly little hands
That move
Around and around
Like a merry-go-round
That *never ever* stops.

TODAY,
Right *now*,
This very moment,
I'm getting off,
So I can
Feel the cool winds
Blow through my hair,
Taste the
Autumn air,
And smell the
Fruit colored leaves
Before they are buried
In the snow.

Come students.
Come with me.

Forget the DO,
It's time to BE.

Teachers' Conference Day

They let me out
They let me out
I can't believe I'm free
No kids today
No kids today
No kids to tire me!

I've left behind
I've left behind
Thirty little souls
I need a rest
I need a break
I think I'm on parole!

Free at last
Free at last
For just a single day
Enjoy the rest
Enjoy the peace
I'll celebrate

Hooray!

The IBTIA Degree

By Kalli Dakos and Sid Cratzbarg

Sid's Three Hairstyles Inspired this Poem
Parted. Unparted. Departed.

I've been
Through rows to groups,
Whole language to phonics,
From thirty-five students
In a classroom to twenty,
And back to thirty-five again,
From principals who believe
In the powers of bureaucracy,
To those where the
Numero Uno
Is always the student,
From parents who show up
For conferences
And class presentations
To those I have never met,
From peer evaluation,
To co-operative learning,
To portfolios,
Student conferences,
Written report cards,
And those on the computer.

I have felt like a magnet,
Pulled back and forth
Between positive and negatives forces
Until I'd forgotten where to stand.

But,
The biggest change
Throughout my teaching career,
And the most heartbreaking by far
Has been on my...
HEAD.

Once my hair
Was lush like a rainforest,
Black as the lead on a pencil,
And wavy as a surfer's dream.

But, with every change
In this ever-changing profession,
My hair turned
From black to gray,
The waves disappeared
And bald spots
Grew in their place
Like a lush rainforest
Lost in the name of progress.

And when my hair is all gone,
And I am as bald as a ping pong ball,
I will officially receive
Not a Master's Degree,
Or a Doctorate,
Not the Principalship of a school,
The Superintendency of a district,
Or a Consultant Laureate,

But the greatest degree
That our noble profession offers –

The IBTIA Degree –
I've Been Through It All!

She Went for the Stars

This poem is dedicated to Christa McAuliffe, the first teacher chosen to travel in space. She died with the rest of the crew when Challenger exploded 73 seconds after launch on January 28, 1986. In memory, I wrote this poem on January 28, 1987.

She was a teacher
In a classroom just like ours,
But she dreamed like a champion
And went for the stars.

And when her craft exploded
In a blazing ball of light,
I saw how dreams inflamed her,
When once they starred her night.

"Why did you keep on dreaming?"
I asked the champions of the past.
"Why did you even bother
In a world where nothing lasts?"

And I wondered why so many
Would still dream of outer space,
Would pick that torch of failure,
Would risk that dangerous place.

But perhaps the torch she gave us
Was the brightest star she sought,
Lighting risks along the journey
We must take despite the cost.

She was a teacher
In a classroom just like ours,
But she passed the torch for dreaming,
That *will* take us to the stars!

Ode to a Librarian

As the heart of a school,
The very soul,
She transforms the pieces
Into a whole.
Hers is a most distinguished role,
As the heart of a school,
The very soul.

How You Live

I often don't hear
The lectures you give.

But my heart
Hears the lessons
You teach me,

By how you live.

Ms. Jones has Cancer

Ms. Jones, our teacher,
Has been sick for awhile.
Even though we're worried
She still makes us smile.

The treatments for cancer
Have taken her hair,
But she makes us laugh
By the wigs that she wears.

One day she's a blonde,
The next a brunette,
Today her hair looks like
The sun when it sets.

One day it's short,
The next it's long,
Today she put a
Ponytail on.

One day it's frizzy,
The next it's straight.
Today it's curly
And sure looks great.

Colors of hair in
All different styles,
And a teacher with cancer
Who still makes us smile.

I'll remember Ms. Jones
Till my own hair turns gray.
I'll remember those wigs
Till the end of my days.

Are There Victories in the End?

by Jan Price

Are there victories in the end?
Did Susie finally make a friend?

Did Katie listen in my class?
Did Joe finish *all* his math?

Did Carlos get himself on track?
Did Mary read her writing back?

Did Madeleine make up with Roy?
Did Joseph laugh with all that joy?

Did Johnny stay put in his seat?
For six years old, this is a feat.

These *are* victories in the end,
Too small for some to comprehend,

And so much joy
    When teachers see,
        How small a victory
            Can really be.

It's Sooooooooooooooooooo Wearisome

Must do
Have to
Get all the work done.
Have to
Must do
Through curriculum.
Must do
Have to
Always on the run.
Have to
Must do
Rushing is no fun.
Must do
Have to
It's so wearisome.
Have to
Must do
What have we become?

STOP!

There's a bird
On the window ledge
Singing to my students,

And a tree
Welcoming
The first blossoms
Of spring.
There's a warm breeze
Telling us to pick
The golden-haired dandelions
That dance on the playground.

TODAY,
I will travel
Beyond the shadows
Of MUST DO
And HAVE TO
Because they've forgotten
How to play
In the sunshine,
And they muffle the words
To the most important
Story of all.

The breeze will hold my hand,
And the dandelions
Will teach me to dance
Once more in the sun,
And I will share
With the children,
As only a real teacher can,
The songs and dances
Of life

TODAY!

Half-Hearted Teachers

We are half-hearted teachers,
Worrying about portfolios
And evaluations
And scores on tests,
When our sacred work
Is about bringing light
To human souls.

We are like mannequins
Who do what we are told
Instead of divine
Queens and Kings
Who know that the
Entire universe
Waits breathlessly,
To see if we carry out
Our mission.

If we let our candles
Become weak
And our flames die out,
How can we possibly
Pass on the light
That is the essence
Of our true being
And our sacred calling
As teachers?

I Heard You Twice the First Time

(Teacher Talking to One Student)

I heard you twice the first time,
Your voice crashed in my ear!
Now take that frog
Back outside,
It shouldn't be in here!

The Greatest Stress

A schedule
That stresses
The meaningless,
At the expense
Of the meaningful.

I Do Not Understand this Planet

The aliens, Starkooses,
From Planet Stark
In the Galazy Veruco,
Landed on Planet Earth.

Their mission was to study
The educational systems
Of Earthlings.

The research scientists
Visited many schools
Before reporting
To their commander.

"Is it true that
Earthling children
Are like our own
Starkoosian children?"
The commander questioned.

"It is true, sir,"
Answered the scientists.

"Are you certain
That Earthling children
Have the same
High level of energy?"
The commander asked.

"Yes, indeed sir.
Some children have
To be calmed down
With medications."

"I see,"
Said the commander.
"I have read that
Earthling teachers
Have twenty-five
Of these children
In a single room
All day.
Is this true?"

"It amazed us too, sir,"
Replied the scientists.
"Some rooms have
Thirty or more children
And only one teacher."

"That's unimaginable,"
Declared the commander.
"Are the teachers robots?"

"No sir,
They are indeed Earthlings.
But many of them suffer
From chronic exhaustion.
Because earthling children,
Like Starkoosian children,
Can be difficult to manage."

"Indeed! Indeed!"
Affirmed the commander.
"Are the schools
The most beautiful buildings
On the planet
Like they are on Stark?"
He asked.

"This surprised us,"
Said the scientists.
"Some schools are
Fine looking buildings
While many others are
Poor and run down."

"I don't understand,"
Exclaimed the commander.
"Is not the greatest value
Placed on children
And their education
As it is on Stark?"

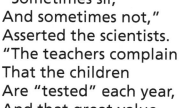

"There are banks
And office buildings
And even stores
Selling clothing
Of far greater worth
Than most schools,"
Replied the scientists.

"I do not understand
This planet,"
Said the commander.
"Are the teachers happy?
Are the children happy?"

"Sometimes sir,
And sometimes not,"
Asserted the scientists.
"The teachers complain
That the children
Are "tested" each year,
And that great value
Is placed on the tests."

"Tested?
Why is a child tested?
He must learn to read and write
And gain knowledge,
But of what use is a test
To an eight-year-old?"
The commander asked.

"To see how he measures
Against other children,"
Declared the scientists.

"But, what does it matter?"
The commander questioned.
"All children are different.
Why would he be compared?"

"We do not understand either,"
The scientists concurred.

"Indeed! Indeed!"
Sighed the commander.
He went to the controls
Of his spaceship
And announced with regret,

"It is time to leave
This planet.
When it comes
To education,
These Earthlings
Have little to teach us."

Learn to Fail

Learn to stumble,
Learn to fall,
Only then will you grow tall.

Learn to try,
Learn to fail,
Only then will your life sail...

Like a ship
Upon the sea
That found the secret to be free.

Don't dodge from waves
Or flee from storms.
Don't stay where it is safe and warm.

But journey
Like a bold strong ship,
That goes through life well-equipped

To ride the waves
And seek new shores,
To go where no one's gone before.

And if your ship
Should hit a rock
And crash and bash and have to stop,

Then take the time
To make repairs
Rest awhile but don't stay there.

And amid the shattered
Decks and sails,
Don't worry that so far you've failed.

Just fix and patch
And build once more,
And continue to your distant shore.

And if you
Lose your way this time,
Seek once more until you find

Your dream come true
At journey's end,
Then rest awhile and dream again.

The ship
That makes it in the night,
Is one that sees its own strong light,

In spite of all
The dangerous rocks
And the chance of getting lost.

The ship
That's not afraid to fail,
Is the only one that's free to sail.

Teachers' Snow Dance

Ba ba ba boom ba
Winter's been too warm,
Ba ba ba boom ba
We're dancing for a storm.

Ba ba ba boom ba
We want the snow to fall,
Ba ba ba boom ba
It's winter after all.

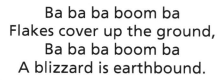

Ba ba ba boom ba
We need a day to rest,
Ba ba ba boom ba
It's snowing from the west!

Ba ba ba boom ba
Flakes cover up the ground,
Ba ba ba boom ba
A blizzard is earthbound.

Ba ba ba boom ba,
The snow has turned to ice,
Ba ba ba boom ba
To add some wintry spice.

Ba ba ba boom ba
With joy the teachers shout!
Ba ba ba boom ba
School has been let out!

A Teacher's Plea

Listen to me when I say,
I NEED MORE HOURS IN A DAY!

Six little hours is not enough
For all the work; it's much too tough,

Spelling, writing, computers and math,
Art, phys ed, and music class.

For adding numbers and taking scores,
Checking assignments; there's always more!

Listen to me when I say,
I NEED MORE HOURS IN A DAY!

Zip a Me

by Eowana Jordan

Zip-A-Dee-Doo-Dah
Zip-A-Dee-A
Zip me a very special day.
Zip me a love boat,
Zip me some fun,
Today I'll be heading for joy in the sun.

Zip-A-Dee-Doo-Dah
Zip-A-Dee-A
Zip me some magic to light up the day.
Zip me some cruising
Zip me some rum
Today my report cards are finally done!

Zip-A-Dee-Doo-Dah
Zip-A-Dee-A,
Zip me some music dancing away,
Zip me some romance
Zip me some sun
Today our holidays have begun!

A Student is Driving Me Crazy,
But I Have Hope...
His House is For Sale!

by Kalli Dakos and Sid Cratzbarg

I pray
I pray
He moves away.
I just can't stand
Another day.

His house
Is taking
Too long to sell.
I have a secret
I won't tell.

Heigh ho
Heigh ho
It's to the bank I go,
A mortgage I'll take,
The payments I'll make.
Heigh ho
Heigh ho
It's to the bank I go.

The Greatest Failure

Time,
My students' precious
Childhood years,
Often devoured
By a schedule
That has little
Respect for
Beauty,
Play,
Celebration,
Joy,
Childhood,
And the healing powers
Of love itself.

Time only for
Assignments,
Marks,
Reports,
Lessons,
Tests
And finally,
Numbers
On papers
That define
Success and failure.

No time for
The Child,
In a world of
Baby executives
Pressured to succeed
At all costs.

And that so-called success,
Is death to childhood,
And the greatest failure of all!

I Touch the Future

Dedicated to the memory of Christa McAuliffe
whose motto as a teacher was "I touch the future."

I plant the seeds
That may grow
Tall and strong and true,
As a gift to the future
That I send with you.

Those precious seeds
I plant with care
For they might grow as dreams,
And when it's time to harvest
To the stars you may have been.

A part of me
Will ride with you
Wherever you may go;
I plant the seed,
You reap a harvest
I may never know.

And somewhere in a future
I may never see,
There will be sounds of laughter
That from the past grew free,
Or music,
Or a story,
Or a dream
Beyond compare,
And somewhere in the magic
My heart will still be there.

For I know
I touch the future
From the past,
Right here,
With you.

Queens and Kings of Imperfection

(Inspired by Kalli Dakos and Tricia Gibbons)

It might not seem
Like we are queens and kings,
But look carefully,
*   And see,*
*   Gloriously crowned,*
*   Beautifully inept,*
*   Marvelously imperfect,*
*   Queens and Kings of Imperfection.*

We leave perfection
To the few
    Who seek
            what cannot be attained,
    Who desire
            what cannot be given,
    Who yearn for
            what cannot be achieved,
And we accept
    Our crowns of imperfection.

We offer this crown to you
For it is the crown of truth,
And joy,
And laughter,
And wonder,
And freedom
From the tyranny
Of trying to be,
    What can never be,
            Was never meant to be,
                    And will never be.

It might not seem
Like we are queens and kings,
But look carefully,
   And see,
         Gloriously crowned,
         Beautifully inept,
         Marvelously imperfect,
         Queens and Kings of Imperfection.

Wear your crown with joy
And reign with the freedom to:
Run in the wind
But come last in the race,
Dance,
With neither grace nor rhythm,
Sing,
Without a tune,
Play baseball,
But rarely hit the ball,
Teach,
But not perfection,
And love,
   Not just the best in you,
   But the sad, weak, discouraged
   And sorry parts, too.

It might not seem
Like we are queens and kings,
But look carefully,
   And see,
         Gloriously crowned,
         Beautifully inept,
         Marvelously imperfect,
         Queens and Kings of Imperfection.

I'll Pat Myself on the Back

by Kalli Dakos and Tricia Gibbons

I survived another amazing day
With *thirty-one* second graders,
One birthday party
With only **thirty** cupcakes,
A firedrill in the rain
Without an umbrella,
And a sick guinea pig
For sharing time

    Soooooooooooooooooooooooooooo…
        I'll pat myself
        On the back
        On the back,
        I'll pat myself
        On the back.

I survived another amazing day
With recess duty
On a muddy playground
Trying to keep two hundred
And fifty-six mud lovers dry
And ending up with brown splotches
All over my new red coat
That I just bought on sale
After watching the price go down
Month after month
For the past *five* months.
The kids called them my
New brown polka-dots,
And wrote a poem about them.

    Soooooooooooooooooooooooooooooo…
        I'll pat myself
        On the back
        On the back,
        I'll pat myself
        On the back.

I survived another amazing day
At a time in history
When teachers are:
        Parents,
        Nurses,
        Psychologists,
        Therapists,
        Entertainers,
        Dieticians,
        Mediators,
        Judges,
        And
        Much
        Much
        More.

Sooooooooooooooooooooooooooooooo…
        I'll pat myself
        On the back
        On the back,
        I'll pat myself
        On the back.

I Sing For

I sing for the teacher who fails
And goes home depressed,
I sing for the courage it takes
To try, yet fail the test.

I sing for all the sadness
And heartaches teachers face,
When they stand up for students,
And pray for acts of grace.

I sing for joy and laughter
But also, sorrow and tears,
The strength to walk in wisdom,
The lessons that last the years.

On the Wings of Imaginaton

On the wings of imagination
We soar
Higher than
Birds in the sky
To other worlds
And galaxies
Still a dream away,
And further still
Into the infinite splendor,
Where we fashion
Stars of our own.

I Heard You Twice the First Time
(Teacher Talking to Herself)

I heard you twice the first time,
You're tired
You're beat
You're low,
You don't want to teach today
Your light is dim and low.

I heard you twice the first time,
Now
Come on
TAKE CONTROL,
Light your candle,
Light your torch,
Light your heart and soul!

I Pray

I pray your elders
Take time to listen
To the stories in your hearts,
So that you will take
Time to listen
To the stories
In their hearts,
When stories
Are all they have left.

I pray
Your elders
Look at you
With awe and wonder and respect
For all that you can become,
So that you will look at them
With awe and wonder and respect
For all that they became.

I pray
Your elders teach
Patience,
Compassion,
And joy
Along with
Reading,
Writing
And arithmetic,
So you will have
Patience for their struggles,
Compassion for their tears,
And joyful places
For them to rest,
In their final years.

I pray your elders
Have time
To share with you
The golden sunlight,
The darkening shadows,
And the truths
That are important
For all time,
So you will see
The glowing candle
Of eternity
In them,
Even though their bodies
Crumble
Like the last leaves
In the moment
Before winter's breath.

I pray
Your elders
Remember to nourish
Your spirits
And souls
So you will remember
They have
Spirits and souls,
When their memories
Are lost in the fogs
Over the rivers
Of yesterday.

I pray
Your elders teach
Wisdom,
Grace,
And love,
For in the brief moment
It takes
A leaf to fall
From a tree,
They
Will pass the
Glowing torch
Of life
To you,

The children of today,

Their leaders,
Their caregivers,
Their hope,
And *their* promise
For tomorrow.

Give Us a J

It won't be here
A day too soon,
The day school ends
Sometime in June!

Teachers everywhere
Give a cheer,
You've nearly survived
Another school year!

Give us a J

J

Give us a U

U

Give us an N

N

Give us an E

E

What does it spell?
JUNE!

Louder!
JUNE!

Loudest!
JUNE!

Yeah! Yeah!

Because of You

There are children
Living sad stormy lives,
Who had moments of
Pure happiness,
Pure childhood,

Because of you!

There are students
Reading
And
Writing
With joy
For the *first* time,

Because of you!

There are children
Realizing
At least for a moment,
They *are* pure gold,

Because of you!

There are students
Dusting off
Forgotten dreams,
And thinking once more
About faraway stars,

Because of you!

All that Counts

A teacher stood at the Pearly Gates,
Her head was bent and low,
She whispered to St. Peter,
"I did my best down there, although…

I never made much money,
No awards did I claim,
Not an Oscar nor an Emmy
Not a single ounce of fame.

Now I have a question
To ask of the divine,
"Were my days in school
Worth all that work and time?"

Saint Peter turned to her and said,
"Come sit with me awhile,
Every moment is on record
Every second with a child.

Let's look at heaven's video
Of your life down on earth,
And we will find the answer
To your value and your worth"

I saw myself in classrooms,
I laughed and cried again,
When St. Peter stopped the video
At a small boy named Ben.

"Your answer," said the Saint,
Is in this one little boy,
A child filled with sorrow,
A teacher filled with joy.

Now, look at all his laughter!
Your love showed him the way!
And that is all that counts,
Here in heaven today!"

Contributors

Sid Cratzbarg
Sid is a former classroom teacher and a primary specialist who has conducted workshops for teachers and students all over Canada and the United States. He feels that teachers can either laugh or cry about classroom life and that joy and humor are always best. He lives in Ottawa, Canada.

Julia Critchfield
Julia has been an elementary teacher and school librarian for 34 years. She teaches children's literature and library classes at the University of Virginia, and is currently working on several exciting manuscripts for children.

Tricia Gibbons
Tricia was a published poet and elementary school teacher in Fairfax, Virginia. She inspired children and teachers to write "from their hearts" and to celebrate the poetry in their lives.

Eowana Jordan
Eowana is a librarian in Prince William County, Virginia and calls herself a "bunhead." She is the mom to two Norwich Terriers (Penelope and Pandora) and the wife to Lenny, a prince among men.

Jan Price
Jan is a former elementary school reading specialist and presently teaches in a court based alternative high school. She is the mother of two college-aged students and lives with her husband in Fairfax, Virginia.

My thanks go to:

* Linda Fletcher of Fredericksburg, Virginia for being the inspiration behind the title of this book.

* Alexandra Dakos, Kathy Sperdakos, Alicia Desmarteau, Betty Sperdakos and Lois Copis for editorial support.

* Gina Marin for coming in at the eleventh hour and helping in more ways than we could have even imagined.

* The teachers and students who are the true inspiration behind these poems.

Other Books by Kalli Dakos

- If You're Not Here, Please Raise Your Hand and Other School Poems
- Don't Read This Book, Whatever You Do! More School Poems
- Mrs. Cole on an Onion Roll and Other School Poems
- Get Out of the Alphabet, Number 2 (Wacky Wednesday Poems)
- The Goof Who Invented Homework and Other School Poems
- The Bug in Teacher's Coffee and Other School Poems
- Put Your Eyes Up Here and Other School Poems
- Our Principal Promised to Kiss a Pig
- The Greatest Magic – Poems for Teachers
- What's There to Write About?

Kalli Dakos has written over 2,000 poems about life in school. Her greatest joy, as a reading specialist, is to help students and teachers fall in love with the drama inside their own classrooms and to capture it in poetry.

She feels that an elementary school has the best stories of all, and she has spent her career celebrating the happy, sad, tragic, silly and joyous moments in classrooms everywhere.

She encourages teachers to "play poetry" and models the process on school visits. Toys like her giant inflatable pig (OUR PRINCIPAL PROMISED TO KISS A PIG) help capture the spirit of childhood, and inspire the most reluctant students to read and write about the school world.

Kalli lives in Ottawa, Ontario, and has an office in Ogdensburg, New York. She was born in Canada, but has lived for twenty-five years in the United States (Virginia, New York and Nevada).

She feels blessed to have had the opportunity to live and work with teachers in two wonderful countries. This book is both inspired by and written for them.

For more information about her books and her school/conference programs visit her website at: www.KalliDakoscom.

Denis Proulx is an award winning children's book illustrator and cartoonist who has illustrated more than thirty children's books. He has always loved to draw, and has studied Illustration and Graphic Design at Algonquin College in Ottawa, Canada.

He lives in the small town of Low, Quebec, where there are more deer than people. It is his Shangri-La away from the hustle and bustle of the city and the place where his creativity is at its best.

You can reach Denis at his studio at www.shangrila-studio.com

Gina Marin is a graphic designer, illustrator and letterpress printer. She graduated from Graphic Design at St. Lawrence College, Kingston Ontario, Canada.

She lives in Ottawa, Ontario where she works in the communications industry and moonlights as an illustrator and letterpress greeting card and stationery designer. Her own line of greeting cards has just been released.

Gina can be reached at www.marinpress.com.

Made in the USA
Las Vegas, NV
14 December 2021